Connection

Published in the United States of America by Cherry Lake Publishing
Ann Arbor, Michigan
www.cherrylakepublishing.com

Reading Adviser: Marla Conn, MS, Ed., Literacy specialist, Read-Ability, Inc.
Book Designer: Jennifer Wahi
Illustrator: Jeff Bane

Photo Credits: ©Sergey Maksienko/Shutterstock, 5; ©Maria Evseyeva/Shutterstock, 7; ©paulaphoto/
Shutterstock, 9; ©Elena Srubina/Shutterstock, 11; ©Brocreative/Shutterstock, 13; ©Amelia Fox/
Shutterstock, 15; ©David Tadevosian/Shutterstock, 17; ©Aaron Amat/Shutterstock, 19; ©Pond's
Memories/Shutterstock, 21; ©Dragon Images/Shutterstock, 23; Cover, 8, 14, 22, Jeff Bane; Various
vector images throughout courtesy of Shutterstock.com

Library of Congress Cataloging-in-Publication Data has been filed and is available at catalog.loc.gov

Printed in the United States of America
Corporate Graphics

About the author: Katie Marsico is the author of more than 200 reference books for children and young adults. She lives with her husband and six children near Chicago, Illinois.

About the illustrator: Jeff Bane and his two business partners own a studio along the American River in Folsom, California, home of the 1849 Gold Rush. When Jeff's not sketching or illustrating for clients, he's either swimming or kayaking in the river to relax.

being mindful

Are you **connected**?

Yes, you're online.

But read the question again.

There's more to it than that.

Being connected is a choice.

We choose to look at feelings more closely.

We **sense** them more deeply.

Connections are what join us.

We're joined to each other.

We're joined to the world around us.

A good place to start is our feelings.

We're more **mindful** of them if we slow down.

We need to **focus** on the present.

What do we feel now?

Connection is also about other people.

We should pause and listen.

It's how we truly get to know them.

We're connected to nature, as well.

The sights and sounds of nature calm us.

What do you love about nature?

Using feelings to connect sounds simple.

But we often move fast.

We don't always make time to be mindful.

People practice slowing down.

They **meditate**.

They do **yoga**.

What do you do to slow down?

To connect with others, we should focus on them.

Setting aside electronics helps.

So does going outside.

Playing a game is a great chance to connect!

Being connected helps us.

We see the bigger picture.

We're part of it.

How can you be mindful today?

glossary

connected (kuh-NEKT-id) joined together

focus (FOH-kuhs) to give your attention to

meditate (MED-ih-tate) to train your mind to relax and focus

mindful (MINDE-ful) aware of your body, mind, and feelings

sense (SENS) to be aware of

yoga (YOH-guh) poses, breathing, and sometimes meditation and chanting that provide balance and good health

index